The Art of Entrepreneurship
Building a business with creativity, vision, and impact

By Tanasa Vlad

CONTENTS

Introduction: The Evolution of Entrepreneurship and its Importance in the Modern World.

Chapter 1: Developing a Vision for Your Business: Setting goals, identifying opportunities and creating a mission statement.

Chapter 2: Unleashing Your Creativity: How to generate new ideas and think outside the box.

Chapter 3: Identifying Your Target Market: Understanding your customers and their needs.

Chapter 4: Crafting a Business Model: Designing a sustainable and profitable business model.

Chapter 5: Building a Team: Assembling the right people to bring your vision to life.

Chapter 6: Raising Capital: Securing funding and financial support for your business.

Chapter 7: Marketing and Branding: Creating a strong brand and effective marketing strategy.

Conclusion: Staying true to your vision, being agile and adaptable in the face of change, and continuing to innovate and grow.

Introduction

The Evolution of Entrepreneurship and its Importance in the Modern World.

Entrepreneurship has come a long way since the days of the merchants and traders of ancient civilizations. Today, the term encompasses a wide range of activities and industries, from tech startups to social enterprises and everything in between. But what exactly is entrepreneurship, and why is it so important in the modern world?

At its core, entrepreneurship is the process of identifying a need or opportunity and creating a new venture to meet that need. It is about innovation and taking risks, often with the goal of creating something that is both economically viable and socially impactful. In a world where technology and globalization have made it easier than ever to start a business, entrepreneurship is more important than ever.

Consider the story of Jane, a young woman who had always been passionate about environmental conservation. After completing her degree in environmental science, she returned to her hometown to find that the local landfill was overflowing and the nearby river was polluted. Despite the lack of local government action, Jane saw this as an opportunity to make a difference.

She set to work researching different waste management methods, and soon discovered an innovative technology that could transform the way that communities dealt with their waste. With the help of a small team of like-minded individuals, she set up her own waste management company, which quickly gained traction and began winning contracts across the region.

Through her business, Jane was able to clean up the river, reduce the landfill burden and create jobs in her community. Her business serves as a shining example of the power of entrepreneurship to create positive change, even in the face of seemingly insurmountable challenges.

Jane's story illustrates the many different facets of entrepreneurship and its importance in the modern world. By recognizing the need for a cleaner environment, she was able to create her own company which not only addressed that need but also created jobs, generated income and had a positive impact on the community. Entrepreneurs like her are not only creating economic value but also making a difference in society. They are a driving force for economic growth and social progress.

In today's fast-paced and constantly evolving world, entrepreneurship has become a vital tool for individuals, communities, and nations to drive progress and create a better future. Entrepreneurs are innovators, risk-takers and creators, and their actions have the power to change the world for the better. Entrepreneurship is not only an important part of the economy, but it is a powerful tool for making a difference in the world.

However, it is important to note that entrepreneurship is not just about starting and growing successful businesses. It is also about a mindset and approach that can be applied to any area of life. Entrepreneurs are problem-solvers, they are able to see opportunities where others see challenges and they are not afraid to try new things. This mindset can be valuable not just for those looking to start their own business, but for anyone looking to make a positive impact in their community, organization or even in their personal life.

Entrepreneurship education and support have also become increasingly important in fostering this mindset and equipping individuals with the necessary skills to succeed as entrepreneurs. Many universities and organizations now offer entrepreneurship programs and resources, providing mentorship, access to funding, and networking opportunities for aspiring entrepreneurs.

Entrepreneurship has been a part of human history since the earliest civilizations. From the merchants and traders of ancient Mesopotamia and Egypt, to the guilds and apprentices of the Middle Ages, to the industrial revolution and the rise of the modern corporation, the practice of entrepreneurship has taken many forms over the centuries.

One of the earliest examples of entrepreneurship can be found in ancient Mesopotamia, where merchants and traders would travel great distances to buy and sell goods, taking advantage of the region's extensive trade networks. The merchants of ancient Egypt also played a significant role in the development of early entrepreneurship. They would build ships and set sail down the Nile to trade with other civilizations, which helped to spread their culture and goods around the world.

During the Middle Ages, guilds and apprenticeships became the norm for business and trade. Guilds were organizations of skilled workers who would come together to protect their trade and to help new members learn the skills they needed to become successful craftsmen. Apprenticeships provided young people with the opportunity to learn a trade or profession under the guidance of experienced masters.

The industrial revolution brought significant changes to the way that businesses were run. The advent of new technologies, such as the steam engine, the cotton gin, and the spinning jenny, allowed entrepreneurs to produce goods on a much larger scale than ever before. This led to the rise of the modern corporation, which allowed multiple investors to pool their resources and take on large-scale projects.

Entrepreneurship continued to evolve in the 20th century, with the rise of the service economy, the introduction of new technologies, and the increasing global interconnectedness. The development of the internet and digital technologies has opened up new opportunities for entrepreneurs to start and grow businesses, and has enabled more people to participate in the global economy.

In the present day, the concept of entrepreneurship has broadened to encompass a wide range of activities and industries. From social entrepreneurship and impact investing, to the sharing economy and the gig economy, the practice of entrepreneurship has become more diverse and inclusive than ever before. This is in part because of the more democratized access to resources, technology and information.

As we look to the future, the field of entrepreneurship is sure to continue evolving. The ongoing technological revolution and the increasing global interconnectedness will bring new opportunities and challenges for entrepreneurs to navigate. But one thing is for sure, the spirit of innovation and the drive to create something new will always be at the heart of entrepreneurship, as it has been throughout history.

Entrepreneurship and small businesses play a crucial role in the global economy. They drive innovation and create jobs, leading to economic growth and development. According to the Small Business Administration (SBA), small businesses account for 44% of U.S. economic activity and create two out of every three new jobs in the country. But the impact of entrepreneurship is not limited to just the United States, it is a global phenomenon.

One of the key ways in which entrepreneurship contributes to the economy is by creating jobs. Small businesses are the largest job creators in the economy, and they often provide jobs with better wages and benefits than larger companies. Furthermore, Small businesses also have a more significant impact on the local communities they are based in, providing jobs, driving economic growth and supporting local infrastructure.

Entrepreneurship also drives innovation. Small businesses are often the first to adopt new technologies, processes, and business models, which leads to increased productivity and economic growth. They also tend to focus on niche markets, which often leads to the creation of new products and services that drive the economy forward.

Entrepreneurship also contributes to economic growth by promoting competition. Small businesses often compete with larger, established companies, which leads to increased productivity and better goods and services for consumers. This competition drives innovation and helps to keep prices low.

Finally, entrepreneurship also contributes to the economy through increased tax revenue. Small businesses often pay higher tax rates than larger companies, and they also generate income for local governments through sales and property taxes.

In conclusion, entrepreneurship and small businesses play a crucial role in the global economy. They drive innovation, create jobs, and promote competition. Their contributions lead to economic growth and development, and also have a positive impact on the local communities they are based in. It is important for governments and private sector to provide an enabling environment for entrepreneurs and small businesses to thrive and for the global economy to keep growing.

Chapter 1

Developing a Vision for Your Business: Setting goals, identifying opportunities and creating a mission statement.

The Importance of Developing a Vision for Your Business

Developing a vision for your business is essential for its success. A vision statement defines the future you want to create for your business, and it serves as a guiding principle that helps you stay focused on what's important. It helps you identify your business's purpose, direction and goals and serves as a compass that helps you navigate the many challenges that arise during the life of a business.

A clear vision helps you to understand what you want to achieve and gives you a sense of direction. Without a vision, you may find yourself aimlessly wandering and making decisions that are not aligned with your goals. A vision statement helps you stay focused on what is truly important and what sets you apart from your competitors. It also helps you to communicate your business's purpose to your employees, partners, and customers.

In addition, a vision statement also serves as a source of inspiration. When you are clear on your vision, you are better able to inspire and motivate your team to work towards it. A vision statement helps to create a sense of purpose and shared goals among your employees, which can lead to increased productivity and a more engaged workforce.

Having a vision for your business is also important for making strategic decisions. A well-defined vision statement will help you evaluate opportunities and make decisions that are in line with your goals. It provides a framework for decision making that can be used to evaluate investment opportunities, partnerships and other key business decisions.

Additionally, having a vision for your business also helps to promote long-term thinking. Without a vision, businesses can get caught up in short-term goals and quick wins, which can lead to a lack of focus on long-term sustainability and growth. A vision statement helps to keep your business's focus on the big picture, and what you want to achieve in the long-term, this will be beneficial in creating a sustainable business model.

Also, with a clear vision, you are better equipped to articulate your value proposition to potential investors, customers, and other stakeholders. With a well-defined vision statement, you can communicate what sets your business apart and what makes it unique in a way that is clear, concise, and compelling. This can help you to attract more investment, customers, and partners, which can fuel growth and success.

Finally, developing a vision statement can be a valuable exercise for the business owner as well. The process of creating a vision statement can help to identify personal goals, and align them with the business goals. It can be a way of looking at the future, and seeing what it is that the owner wants to achieve, not just for the business but for themselves as well.

A short story that illustrates the importance of developing a vision for your business is that of John, a young entrepreneur who had always been passionate about technology. He had spent years working for other companies, but he always dreamed of starting his own business. So, he decided to take the plunge and start his own tech company.

At first, things were going well. John had secured a few contracts and was able to bring on a small team of employees. However, as the business grew, John found himself facing a number of challenges. He found himself constantly putting out fires and reacting to the demands of customers and partners, without a clear sense of direction.

One day, John sat down and realized that he needed to step back and think about where he wanted to take his business. He spent some time thinking about his passion for technology, his goals for the future, and the challenges he faced as a business owner. Through this process, he developed a vision statement for his business: "To create innovative technology solutions that help businesses thrive in a digital world."

With this vision statement in place, John was able to make strategic decisions that aligned with his goals and purpose. He began to focus on creating products that met the specific needs of his target market, rather than trying to be all things to all people.

Setting Business Goals: Understanding what you want to achieve

Setting clear and measurable business goals is essential for the success of any venture. Without specific goals, it can be difficult to know what you want to achieve and how to measure progress. Goals provide a roadmap for success and help you stay focused on what's important.

When setting business goals, it's essential to first identify the overall vision and mission of the business. This will help to ensure that your goals align with the overall direction of the company. Then, your goals should be specific, measurable, attainable, relevant, and time-bound (SMART).

For example, instead of simply stating a goal to "increase sales," a SMART goal would be to "increase sales by 15% within the next quarter by expanding our market reach through targeted advertising campaigns." This specific goal is measurable and has a clear target and timeline, making it easier to track progress and determine if the goal has been achieved.

It's also important to set goals for different areas of the business, such as sales, marketing, and operations. This can help you to focus on specific areas that need improvement and identify any bottlenecks that might be preventing you from achieving your overall vision.

Another important step is setting up a process to track your goals, this can be done through creating a dashboard or by using a goal management software. This will help you to monitor progress and make adjustments as necessary. You should also review your goals regularly, this will help you to stay on track, identify any obstacles and make adjustments if necessary.

Another short story to illustrate the importance of setting clear business goals, consider the case of Sarah, who owned a small retail store. When she first started her business, she didn't set any specific goals for herself or her business. She simply worked hard, hoping that her efforts would pay off.

As time passed, Sarah noticed that her business wasn't growing as quickly as she had hoped. She was having trouble attracting new customers and wasn't making as much money as she needed to sustain her business.

Frustrated and unsure of what to do next, Sarah decided to take a step back and assess her situation. She realized that she didn't have a clear idea of what she wanted to achieve with her business. She had been working hard, but without specific goals, she didn't know if her efforts were paying off.

With the help of a business coach, Sarah began to set specific, measurable goals for her business. She set targets for increasing sales, attracting new customers, and improving her marketing efforts. She also developed a plan to track her progress and make adjustments as necessary.

As Sarah started to focus on achieving her goals, she noticed a significant change in her business. Her sales began to increase, and she was able to attract new customers. Her marketing efforts were also more effective, and she was able to reach more people. Sarah's business began to grow, and she felt more confident in her ability to achieve her vision.

Identifying Opportunities: Analyzing the market and identifying areas for growth

Identifying opportunities for growth is a crucial step for any business looking to expand and achieve success. The ability to spot new opportunities and capitalize on them can be the difference between a business that thrives and one that struggles.

One of the first steps in identifying opportunities is to thoroughly analyze the market. This involves researching the industry, understanding the competitive landscape, and identifying trends and changes in consumer behavior. By gaining a deep understanding of the market, you can identify areas where there is a demand for products or services that your business could meet.

You should also look for gaps in the market, these gaps could be a new product or service that is not being offered by your competitors, or a new market or geographic location where there is a need for your products or services. Also, you should look for untapped customer segments or new channels to reach customers that are not being served by competitors.

It's also important to keep an eye out for emerging technologies or changes in regulations that could open up new opportunities for your business. For instance, the rise of e-commerce has created new opportunities for businesses to reach customers online, and the increasing focus on sustainability has created opportunities for businesses that offer eco-friendly products or services.

In addition, you should also take into account internal factors, such as the skills and expertise of your team, and any existing resources, such as equipment or software that could be used to create new opportunities.

Another important aspect to consider when identifying opportunities is to not limit yourself to what's currently in your field. Sometimes, opportunities can come from areas or industries that may seem unrelated to your business. It is important to be open to new ideas and perspectives, and to be willing to explore opportunities that may not be immediately obvious.

Also, actively seeking out new opportunities can be valuable. Networking, attending industry events and conferences, and reaching out to potential partners or collaborators can help you to identify new opportunities that you might not have been aware of otherwise.

Another way to identify opportunities is to gather customer feedback and insights, this can be done through conducting surveys, focus groups or through other means of data collection. This can help you to identify unmet needs or pain points that your business could address.

In addition, having a culture of innovation and encouraging experimentation and risk-taking within your team can also help you to identify new opportunities. Encouraging your team members to come up with new ideas, and testing and iterating on them can lead to the development of new products, services or even business models.

Another way to identify opportunities is by looking at your competitors. Analyzing what your competitors are doing well and what they are missing can help you to identify opportunities for your own business. By understanding the strengths and weaknesses of your competition, you can position yourself differently and target areas where your competitors are not serving the customers well. Also, you can find the gap in the market and create unique selling points that can distinguish you from your competitors.

Additionally, paying attention to customer complaints and negative feedback can also help you identify opportunities. By listening to what customers are not happy with, you can identify areas of improvement and address those in a way that sets your business apart.

To identify opportunities, It's important to keep a pulse on what is happening in your industry and in the world around you. Following industry news, reading publications and publications, and attending trade shows and events will help you stay informed and aware of trends and potential opportunities.

Understanding Your Customers: Identifying the needs of your target market

Understanding your customers is essential for the success of any business. It allows you to identify their needs and tailor your products or services to meet those needs, which can lead to increased customer satisfaction and loyalty.

One of the first steps in understanding your customers is to identify your target market. This involves defining the specific group of people that your business is trying to reach, and understanding their characteristics, such as demographics, behavior patterns, and pain points.

Once you have a clear understanding of your target market, you can begin to research their needs and preferences. This can be done through a variety of methods such as surveys, interviews, focus groups, and social media listening.

It's also important to pay attention to the feedback your customers give you, both positive and negative. This can provide valuable insights into what they like and dislike about your products or services, and what changes they would like to see. This feedback can be used to improve your offerings and create new products or services that meet the needs of your customers.

In addition, it's important to keep an eye on your customers' behavior. By monitoring how they interact with your products or services, you can gain insight into how they use them and identify areas for improvement.

SWOT Analysis: Assessing the strengths, weaknesses, opportunities and threats of your business

SWOT analysis is a strategic planning tool used to evaluate the strengths, weaknesses, opportunities, and threats involved in a business or project. The acronym SWOT stands for Strengths, Weaknesses, Opportunities, and Threats.

Strengths refer to the unique features or capabilities of a business that give it an advantage over its competitors. This could include things like a strong brand, proprietary technology, or a highly skilled workforce.

Weaknesses refer to the areas in which a business is lacking or in which its competitors have an advantage. This could include things like a lack of funding, a weak market position, or a shortage of skilled employees.

Opportunities refer to external factors that a business can capitalize on to gain a competitive advantage. This could include things like market trends, technological advancements, or changes in consumer behavior.

Threats refer to external factors that could potentially harm a business, such as new regulations, increased competition, or economic downturns.

By conducting a SWOT analysis, a business can identify its key strengths and weaknesses, as well as potential opportunities and threats. This information can then be used to develop a strategic plan to capitalize on strengths and opportunities, while addressing weaknesses and threats.

Conducting a SWOT analysis typically involves the following steps:

1. Gather information: Collect data on your business, including internal factors (strengths and weaknesses) and external factors (opportunities and threats). This can be done through research, interviews with employees and stakeholders, and analysis of financial and performance metrics.
2. Identify strengths: Look for unique features or capabilities that give your business an advantage over its competitors. These could include things like a strong brand, proprietary technology, or a highly skilled workforce.
3. Identify weaknesses: Identify areas in which your business is lacking or in which its competitors have an advantage. These could include things like a lack of funding, a weak market position, or a shortage of skilled employees.
4. Identify opportunities: Look for external factors that your business can capitalize on to gain a competitive advantage. These could include things like market trends, technological advancements, or changes in consumer behavior.
5. Identify threats: Identify external factors that could potentially harm your business, such as new regulations, increased competition, or economic downturns.
6. Create a plan: Use the information gathered in the SWOT analysis to develop a strategic plan to

capitalize on strengths and opportunities, while addressing weaknesses and threats.
7. Monitor progress: Once the plan is in motion, track the progress and make updates if needed. Also, be open to any new change that could affect your SWOT analysis.

It could be helpful to involve multiple parties such as employees, managers, stakeholders, and experts in your industry in order to have a diverse view and gain more insight. And also, it's important to repeat the process periodically to adapt to changes in the internal and external environment.

Creating a Mission Statement: Defining the purpose and values of your business

A mission statement is a brief statement that defines the purpose and values of a business. It communicates the company's overall strategy, its goals, and the customers it serves. It serves as a guiding principle for the company's actions and decision-making, and is often used to align employees and stakeholders with the company's vision.

Creating a mission statement typically involves the following steps:

1. Define your company's purpose: Ask yourself why your company exists and what it hopes to accomplish. This could be anything from providing a needed product or service to creating jobs in the community or making a positive impact on the world.
2. Identify your target customers: Who are the customers you serve and what needs do they have? Understanding your target market will help you identify how you can best serve them.
3. Outline your values: Consider the values that drive your company's decision-making and behavior. These could include things like integrity, innovation, or social responsibility.
4. Draft a statement: Use the information gathered in the previous steps to draft a statement that encapsulates your company's purpose, target customers, and values. The statement should be brief, clear, and easy to understand.
5. Review and refine: Share the draft statement with key stakeholders and employees and gather feedback. Use this feedback to refine the statement until it accurately represents the company's mission.
6. Communicate it: Once the statement is finalized, share it widely with employees, customers, partners, and other stakeholders. It should be easily accessible, visible, and reinforced regularly across internal and external communications.

The mission statement should be a living document that aligns with the company's vision and evolves as the company's goals and objectives change over time. It should be reviewed regularly and updated as necessary to ensure that it remains relevant and aligned with the company's current strategy.

Building a Business Model: Designing a sustainable and profitable business model

A business model is the approach a company takes to generate revenue and create value for its customers. It outlines how the company will make money and how it will provide value to its customers. Building a sustainable and profitable business model requires careful consideration of a number of factors, including the company's value proposition, target market, revenue streams, and cost structure.

Building a business model typically involves the following steps:

1. Define your value proposition: Clearly identify what unique value your business provides to its customers, and how it solves their problems or meets their needs. This could include things like quality, price, convenience, or innovation.

2. Identify your target market: Clearly define the specific group of customers you are targeting, and understand their needs, behavior, and buying habits. This will help you identify the best ways to reach and serve them.
3. Develop revenue streams: Determine how your business will make money. This could include things like selling products or services, advertising, or licensing your technology. Be sure to consider the scalability and sustainability of your revenue streams over time.
4. Create a cost structure: Identify and estimate all the costs associated with your business, including both fixed and variable costs. Identify how these costs will be covered, and how they will change as your business scales.
5. Test and refine: Test your business model with a small group of customers to see if it works as expected. Use feedback to refine and improve your business model.
6. Adapt and evolve: As you learn more about your customers and the market, be prepared to adapt and evolve your business model. Be open to new opportunities and be flexible to pivot to a new approach if the current one isn't sustainable or profitable.

A well-designed business model should be sustainable, adaptable, and aligned with the company's overall strategy. It should clearly identify how the company will create value for its customers, generate revenue, and achieve profitability. Additionally, in today's fast-paced market, a business model should be continuously evaluated, and adjusted as needed to ensure its viability in the face of new opportunities and emerging threats.

Developing a Business Plan: Creating a roadmap for success

A business plan is a written document that outlines the strategy, goals, and operations of a business. It serves as a roadmap for success, providing a clear picture of the company's vision and how it plans to achieve its objectives. A business plan is often used to secure funding from investors or to guide the decision-making of the company's management team.

Developing a business plan typically involves the following steps:

1. Define your business: Clearly describe what your business does, what products or services it offers, and what problem it solves for customers.

2. Research the market: Conduct a thorough analysis of your target market, including the size of the market, the target customer demographics, and the current competition.
3. Develop a marketing strategy: Identify how you plan to reach and persuade your target market to buy your products or services.
4. Identify financial projections: Develop financial projections, including projected income statements, cash flow statements, and balance sheets for at least the next five years.
5. Describe management and organization: Outline the organizational structure of your business, including the key roles and responsibilities of team members and advisors.
6. Include any supporting documents: Include any relevant documents, such as resumes of key team members, product and service descriptions, letters of intent from suppliers or partners, and copies of leases or purchase agreements.
7. Review and revise: Review the plan with your management team, advisors, and any potential investors or partners. Make revisions as necessary, and make sure your business plan accurately reflects your company's vision, mission, and strategy.

A business plan should be reviewed regularly, and should be updated as the company's objectives and strategies change over time. It's a living document that can evolve as the business grows and adapts. The plan should also reflect realistic goals and set realistic milestones to achieve them, also, it should be well-researched, well-written and easy to understand, in order to make it a useful tool for guiding the decision-making process and securing funding or investment.

Let me tell you a story. Sophia had always dreamed of starting her own business, and after years of working in the corporate world, she decided to take the leap and start her own company. She was determined to create a sustainable and profitable business model, and knew that the key to success would be to develop a comprehensive business plan.

Sophia began by defining her business, a line of all-natural skincare products. She knew that the skincare market was crowded, but she was confident that her products were truly unique and could offer real value to customers. She conducted a thorough market research and identified her target customer demographic, young and health-conscious women who were looking for natural and sustainable skincare options.

Next, Sophia developed a marketing strategy to reach her target customers and set out to create a comprehensive financial plan. She worked with an accountant to develop projections for income statements, cash flow statements, and balance sheets for the next five years. She also outlined the organizational structure of her business, including the key roles and responsibilities of her team members.

With all the information gathered, Sophia set to work on crafting her business plan. She spent countless hours reviewing and refining her plan, making sure that it was well-researched, well-written and easy to understand. She shared the plan with her management team, advisors, and potential investors, and received positive feedback and support.

Armed with her business plan, Sophia was able to secure funding and start her business. She was able to get a clear understanding of the company's vision, mission and strategy, and how to reach the goals and milestones set by the business.

As her business grew, Sophia continued to review and update her business plan, making sure that it reflected the company's evolving objectives and strategies. Her business became a great success, and she was able to help many people improve their skin's health.

Years went by and Sophia became a respected figure in the skincare industry, her business continued to grow, and she was able to open up multiple branches across the country. Her business plan served as a roadmap for her company's success, and she knew that she couldn't have done it without it.

Setting Actionable Objectives and Key Results: Setting concrete and measurable goals

Setting actionable objectives and key results (OKRs) is a framework for setting concrete and measurable goals that align with a company's overall strategy. It is a goal-setting method used to help organizations achieve their objectives by providing a clear direction and focus for employees and teams. OKRs are a powerful tool for measuring progress, promoting accountability, and driving performance.

The process of setting OKRs typically involves the following steps:

1. Define your overall objectives: Identify the high-level goals that align with your company's overall strategy and vision. These should be ambitious and specific.
2. Break down objectives into key results: Break down each objective into specific and measurable key results. These are the outcomes that need to be achieved in order to reach the objective.
3. Set targets and timelines: Establish targets and timelines for achieving each key result. These should be ambitious but realistic.
4. Assign ownership: Assign ownership of each key result to an individual or team within the organization. This promotes accountability and ownership for achieving results.
5. Monitor and track progress: Regularly monitor and track progress against key results. Use this data to make adjustments and improve performance.
6. Review and revise: Review and revise OKRs on a regular basis. This ensures that they remain aligned with the company's overall strategy and that progress is being made towards achieving objectives.

OKRs can be set at the organization, team, and individual level. The key is to make sure they are aligned and support one another, so that everyone is working towards a common goal.

Additionally, OKRs should be SMART - Specific, Measurable, Achievable, Relevant, Time-bound - to ensure that they are effective and can be used to track progress and measure success.

Setting OKRs can be a powerful way to align the efforts of an organization and drive performance. They provide a clear direction and focus, and when properly implemented, they can help organizations achieve their objectives.

To better illustrate the process, let's consider a company that wants to increase their online sales. Here's an example of how they might set OKRs:

Objective: Increase online sales by 30% within the next quarter.

Key Results:

1. Increase website traffic by 15% through targeted advertising and search engine optimization (SEO) strategies.
2. Improve website conversion rate by 10% through redesigning the checkout process and offering free shipping.
3. Increase repeat customer rate by 5% through implementing a loyalty program.

Targets and Timelines:

1. Increase website traffic by 15% within the next quarter.
2. Improve website conversion rate by 10% within the next quarter.
3. Increase repeat customer rate by 5% within the next quarter.

Assign Ownership:

1. Website traffic - Marketing team
2. Website conversion rate - E-commerce team
3. Repeat customer rate - Customer service team

By setting OKRs, the company has a clear, measurable and actionable plan to increase their online sales. The teams are aware of their goals and what they need to achieve, and by regularly monitoring and tracking progress, they can make adjustments and improve their performance along the way. Reviewing and revising OKRs on a regular basis allows the company to ensure that the goals remain aligned with their overall strategy and that they are making progress towards achieving their objectives.

OKRs are powerful tool that can be used to align efforts of the organization and drive performance in a specific direction. It's essential to keep in mind that OKRs should be flexible and open to change, as the market and company's circumstances can change, therefore it should adapt and adjust accordingly.

Making Your Vision a Reality: Putting your vision into action and monitoring progress

Making a vision a reality requires a clear plan and commitment to taking action. It's not enough to simply have a vision, it's important to put that vision into action in order to achieve it. A clear plan that outlines how the vision will be achieved, and regular monitoring of progress, will help keep the company on track and ensure that the vision is being realized.

The process of making your vision a reality typically involves the following steps:

1. Define your vision: Clearly articulate what your vision is, and what it means for the company. Be specific, ambitious and make sure it aligns with the overall strategy of the organization.
2. Develop a plan: Create a detailed plan that outlines the steps needed to achieve the vision. The plan should include specific goals, timelines, and the resources required to achieve them.

3. Allocate resources: Identify and allocate the resources needed to achieve the vision, including people, money, and time.
4. Communicate the vision: Share the vision with everyone in the organization, so that everyone understands the company's direction, and how their work fits in.
5. Take action: Implement the plan and take action towards achieving the vision.
6. Monitor progress: Regularly monitor progress towards achieving the vision. Use data and metrics to track progress and measure success.
7. Reflect and adjust: Reflect on progress and make adjustments as needed to ensure the vision is being realized.

It's important to keep in mind that making a vision a reality is an iterative process, the vision and plan should be continuously monitored and adapted as needed to ensure that the company is on track and moving in the right direction. Also, it's crucial to involve everyone in the company in the process, by communicating the vision and involving employees and stakeholders, everyone in the organization can work together to achieve the common goal.

Additionally, it's important to remember that a vision is not a one-time event, but rather an ongoing process that needs to be nurtured and nurtured to ensure that the company continues to innovate and evolve over time.

Chapter 2

Unleashing Your Creativity: How to generate new ideas and think outside the box.

The Power of Mindfulness: Understanding how mindfulness practices can help open the mind to new ideas and perspectives

The power of mindfulness is the ability to open the mind to new ideas and perspectives by becoming more aware of the present moment and breaking free from the constraints of past experiences and preconceptions. Mindfulness practices, such as meditation and journaling, can help individuals tap into their inner creativity by fostering greater awareness and focus.

One of the key benefits of mindfulness is that it helps to reduce stress and anxiety, which can often impede creativity. When we are stressed or anxious, our mind is in a constant state of fight or flight, making it difficult to focus on the present moment or come up with new ideas. Mindfulness practices help to calm the mind and body, making it easier to focus and think more clearly.

Mindfulness also helps to increase self-awareness, which is essential for creativity. By becoming more aware of our thoughts, feelings, and emotions, we can better understand what drives us, what holds us back, and what we are truly passionate about. This self-awareness allows us to break free from limiting beliefs and see things from new perspectives.

Mindfulness practices also help to increase cognitive flexibility, or the ability to shift perspective and think about problems and ideas in different ways. By focusing on the present moment, we can let go of preconceptions and biases, allowing us to explore new and unconventional ideas.

In order to benefit from the power of mindfulness, it's important to make it a regular practice. Setting aside time each day to meditate or journal, for example, can help to establish a regular mindfulness routine. Incorporating mindfulness practices into your daily routine can also help to reduce stress, improve focus and boost overall well-being which will open the mind to new ideas and perspectives.

Breaking Out of the Box: Understanding and overcoming limiting beliefs that hold us back

Limiting beliefs are preconceived notions or self-imposed restrictions that hold us back from reaching our full potential. These beliefs can take many forms, such as "I'm not creative," "I'm not good enough," or "I'll never be able to achieve that." They can be deeply ingrained and hard to recognize, but they can have a powerful impact on our ability to generate new ideas and think outside the box.

To understand and overcome limiting beliefs, it's important to first become aware of them. One way to do this is to pay attention to your thoughts and emotions. When faced with a challenge or a new idea, pay attention to your initial reactions.

Are there any thoughts or beliefs that hold you back from exploring the idea further?

Another way to identify limiting beliefs is to consider your past experiences. Have you had experiences in the past that may have led you to adopt certain beliefs about yourself or your abilities? For example, if you received negative feedback about your creativity in the past, it may have led you to believe that you're not creative.

Once you've identified your limiting beliefs, it's important to challenge them. Ask yourself, "Is this belief really true? What evidence do I have to support it?" This process can help you to see that your beliefs may not be accurate, and to come up with a new perspective.

Additionally, it's important to practice reframing, This is the process of changing the way we interpret things, or looking at things from a different perspective. Instead of focusing on what is holding you back, focus on what you can do to move forward.

Another effective strategy is to take action, even if it means taking small steps and experimenting with new ideas, it's a way to break out of your comfort zone and try new things.

Lastly, surrounding yourself with supportive people, people who will encourage and inspire you to pursue your goals, can be a powerful way to overcome limiting beliefs.

Breaking out of the box and overcoming limiting beliefs requires awareness, commitment, and a willingness to take action. It can be a challenging process, but by understanding the nature of limiting beliefs, and using techniques such as challenging, reframing, and taking action, individuals can begin to break free from these constraints and tap into their full creative potential.

It's also important to remember that limiting beliefs are not permanent, they can be changed and new beliefs can be formed. By consistently working on breaking out of limiting beliefs, and replacing them with more empowering ones, individuals can improve their ability to generate new ideas and think outside the box.

It's also essential to understand that even when we have overcome some limiting beliefs, new ones may appear, so it's an ongoing process of self-awareness and self-improvement.

Here are five potential ways to break out of the box and tap into your creative potential:

1. Challenge your assumptions: Take the time to question your assumptions and preconceptions. Are they based on fact or are they limiting beliefs? Challenge your assumptions and be open to new perspectives.
2. Embrace failure: Failure is an inevitable part of the creative process. Embrace failure as an opportunity to learn and grow. Instead of being discouraged by failure, see it as an opportunity to gain new insights and try again.
3. Embrace experimentation and play: Experimentation and play are powerful tools for breaking out of the box. Allow yourself the freedom to explore new ideas and try new things, even if they may seem unconventional.
4. Learn from others: Seek out diverse perspectives, listen and learn from others who have different experiences, backgrounds, and perspectives. This can help to expand your own perspective and generate new ideas.
5. Take action: Putting your ideas into action is an essential step in breaking out of the box. Even if the idea may seem uncertain or untested, taking action allows you to test and refine your ideas and learn from the experience.

Breaking out of the box requires a shift in perspective, a willingness to take risks, and a commitment to taking action. By embracing failure, experimentation and play, learning from others, and challenging assumptions, you can break free from constraints and tap into your full creative potential. It's essential to remember that breaking out of the box is an ongoing process and new opportunities and perspectives can always be found.

Exploring new perspectives: the importance of diverse perspectives in idea generation

Exploring new perspectives is crucial for idea generation, as diverse perspectives bring a wide range of experiences, perspectives, and ideas that can lead to more innovative and creative solutions. Diverse perspectives can come from people with different backgrounds, cultures, and experiences, and including them in the idea generation process can lead to more inclusive and effective solutions.

One of the benefits of exploring diverse perspectives is that it helps to challenge assumptions and biases. When we are surrounded by people with similar backgrounds and experiences, it can be easy to fall into groupthink and only consider a narrow range of solutions. Diverse perspectives can help to broaden the range of ideas and solutions, and challenge assumptions that might have been taken for granted.

Another advantage is that diverse perspectives can also help to identify new opportunities and unmet needs. People from different backgrounds and cultures may have different experiences and insights that can help to identify new opportunities that might have been overlooked by a homogenous group.

In order to benefit from diverse perspectives, it's important to actively seek them out. This can involve reaching out to a diverse range of people, encouraging participation and input from a wide range of individuals, and creating an inclusive and safe environment where everyone feels comfortable sharing their ideas.

Additionally, it's important to consider diversity in all aspects, not only in regards to race, ethnicity or gender, but also thinking about diversity in terms of age, education, work experience, expertise, and personal beliefs. Each of these factors can bring unique perspectives and ideas to the table.

It's also important to be aware of and address any unconscious biases that may be present. Unconscious biases are learned attitudes or stereotypes that unconsciously influence our thoughts and actions. Unconscious biases can prevent people from fully valuing and benefiting from diverse perspectives, and it's essential to recognize them and make a conscious effort to overcome them.

Daniel was a young entrepreneur who had recently started his own business. He was passionate about his product and was determined to make it a success. However, as he began to develop his business plan and start building his team, he quickly realized that he was struggling to come up with new and innovative ideas.

He knew that he needed to find a way to break out of his current mindset and think more creatively. He decided to reach out to a mentor for advice and was introduced to the concept of exploring new perspectives through diversity.

Daniel realized that his team was homogeneous, and he was not actively seeking out diverse perspectives. He decided to make a conscious effort to diversify his team and started by recruiting individuals from different backgrounds, cultures and experiences. He also made sure to create an inclusive environment where everyone felt comfortable sharing their ideas and perspectives.

By actively seeking out diverse perspectives, Daniel's team was able to challenge assumptions and biases that they had previously taken for granted. They were able to identify new opportunities and generate new and innovative ideas that they would have otherwise missed.

Daniel also made a point of encouraging experimentation and play among his team. He provided them with the resources and support they needed to experiment with new ideas, even if they were unconventional or unproven.

As a result, Daniel's business began to thrive. He had found a way to break out of his current mindset and tap into his full creative potential, thanks to the power of diverse perspectives. He has noticed that his team had a more positive mindset, and they were more willing to take risks and try new things, which led to the company's growth and success.

Daniel had learned that the key to success was to actively seek out and value diverse perspectives. He understood that diversity and inclusivity in the workplace can lead to greater creativity, problem-solving, and innovation.

Play and experimentation: the importance of play and experimentation in idea generation

Play and experimentation are essential elements of idea generation, as they allow individuals to explore new and unconventional ideas, think outside the box, and tap into their full creative potential. Play and experimentation provide opportunities for risk-taking, testing new ideas, and learning from the process.

One of the key benefits of play and experimentation is that it fosters creativity. Play allows individuals to explore new ideas and concepts in a relaxed and non-threatening environment. Experimentation, on the other hand, allows individuals to test their ideas and see what works and what doesn't, leading to a deeper understanding of the subject matter and new insights.

Play and experimentation also help to break free from limiting beliefs and constraints. Play allows individuals to think freely and come up with new ideas without the pressure of success or failure, while experimentation allows individuals to test new ideas and concepts without the fear of failure.

Another benefit of play and experimentation is that it promotes a growth mindset, which is the belief that abilities can be developed through effort and learning. When individuals engage in play and experimentation, they are more likely to embrace challenges and see them as opportunities to learn and grow.

In order to benefit from the power of play and experimentation, it's important to incorporate them into your daily routine. This can involve setting aside time each day for play or experimentation, or incorporating them into your work and personal life in small ways. It's also important to give yourself the freedom to explore new ideas and concepts, even if they may seem unconventional.

To put this into practice, Daniel decided to integrate play and experimentation into his team's weekly routine. He designated one day of the week as "play day" where the team was encouraged to come up with new ideas, and experiment with different concepts, in a relaxed and non-threatening environment. He also gave them the freedom to explore new ideas, even if they seemed unconventional or unproven.

The team quickly embraced this new approach, and they started to generate a wide range of new and innovative ideas. The play day also helped to break down the hierarchies and created a more collaborative and open environment, where team members were encouraged to share their ideas without fear of failure.

Daniel also noticed that this play and experimentation approach helped to increase team's motivation and creativity, and helped them develop a growth mindset. They were more willing to take risks, and they were open to learning from their failures.

Furthermore, by experimenting with different concepts, the team was able to identify new opportunities, that they would have otherwise missed. This led to the development of new products and services that they would have never thought of before.

As a result, Daniel's business continued to grow and flourish, and he knew that it was all thanks to the power of play and experimentation. He understood that the key to success was to create a culture of experimentation and play within the organization, and to embrace a growth mindset.

In short, play and experimentation are key elements in idea generation, they allow individuals to be more creative, take risks and learn from their failures. Incorporating play and experimentation into your routine and creating a culture of experimentation and play within your organization can be beneficial for the business growth and success.

Putting it into action: Developing a plan for idea generation and implementation

Once you understand the importance of diverse perspectives, mindfulness, breaking out of limiting beliefs, play and experimentation, the next step is to develop a plan for idea generation and implementation. This plan should outline the steps you will take to tap into your full creative potential and turn your ideas into action.

Here are a few key steps you can take to put your plan into action:

1. Set clear goals and objectives: Before you begin generating ideas, it's important to have a clear understanding of what you're trying to achieve. Set specific and measurable goals and objectives that align with your overall business strategy.
2. Build a diverse team: Build a team that includes individuals with diverse backgrounds, cultures, and experiences. Encourage participation and input from a wide range of team members, and create an inclusive and safe environment where everyone feels comfortable sharing their ideas.
3. Encourage play and experimentation: Create an environment that promotes play and experimentation. Encourage team members to explore new and unconventional ideas, and provide the resources and support they need to experiment and test new concepts.
4. Monitor progress and adapt: Develop a system for monitoring progress and gathering feedback. Use this information to adapt and adjust your approach as needed.
5. Implement and execute: Once you have a solid plan in place, it's important to execute it effectively. Develop a clear plan of action and assign specific responsibilities to team members.

Make sure everyone is aware of the plan and their role in it.
6. Continuously evaluate: Continuously evaluate and analyze the performance of your plan, see if it's working well or not, if not make necessary changes and adjustments to improve the process.

In summary, developing a plan for idea generation and implementation is an essential step to turning your ideas into action. By setting clear goals and objectives, building a diverse team, encouraging play and experimentation, monitoring progress, executing effectively and continuously evaluating the plan, individuals and organizations can tap into their full creative potential and achieve their goals.

Chapter 3

Identifying Your Target Market: Understanding your customers and their needs.

Understanding your target market

Understanding your target market is a crucial step in developing a successful business strategy. It involves identifying and researching the specific group of people that you aim to sell your products or services to. By understanding your target market, you can create products and services that meet their specific needs, develop more effective marketing strategies, and create a more engaged customer base.

To begin understanding your target market, you first need to identify specific characteristics and demographics. This might include factors such as age, gender, income, location, and lifestyle. This information can be gathered through various research methods such as customer surveys, focus groups, and market analysis.

Once you have a general understanding of your target market, you can then segment it to identify sub-groups within your audience. This might include different segments with different needs or characteristics. For example, you may have one segment that is price-sensitive and another that is willing to pay a premium for a higher-quality product.

It's also important to understand the specific needs and desires of your target market. This includes understanding the customer journey, pain points, and the benefits and features that customers are looking for in a product or service. Conducting customer research and gathering customer feedback can provide valuable insights into customer needs.

Once you have a deep understanding of your target market, you can then develop a positioning and messaging strategy that effectively communicates the value of your product or service to your target market. This includes differentiating your product or service from the competition, creating a unique selling proposition, and developing messaging that resonates with your target market.

5 ways to understand your target market:

1. Conduct Market Research: One of the most effective ways to understand your target market is through market research. This can include surveys, focus groups, and interviews with potential customers to gather information about their demographics, needs, and buying habits. Market research can also include analyzing industry trends and competitors to gain a better understanding of the market landscape.
2. Analyze Customer Data: Gather data on your current customers through sales and marketing campaigns. Analyze the data to identify patterns and trends, such as demographics, location, and purchase history. This can provide valuable insights into your target market and help you to make informed decisions about your marketing strategy.

3. Use Social Media Listening: Use social media listening tools to track and analyze conversations about your brand, products, and industry on social media. This can provide insights into what your target market is saying about your brand and the issues that are important to them.
4. Create Personas: Create detailed personas of your ideal customers. Personas are fictional characters that represent your target market, and they help to provide a more concrete understanding of your target market. Personas include information on demographics, interests, needs, and pain points.
5. Test and Experiment: Experiment with different marketing strategies and promotions to see what resonates with your target market. Use testing and experimentation to gather data on customer preferences and behavior, which can help you make more informed decisions about your target market.

In summary, understanding your target market is crucial to developing a successful business strategy. Market research, data analysis, social media listening, creating personas, and testing and experimenting are all effective ways to gain a deeper understanding of your target market. By using these methods, you can gain valuable insights into your target market and make informed decisions about your marketing and product development strategies.

Defining your target market

Defining your target market is an essential step in developing a successful business strategy. It involves identifying and researching the specific group of people that you aim to sell your products or services to. By defining your target market, you can create products and services that meet their specific needs, develop more effective marketing strategies, and create a more engaged customer base.

To begin defining your target market, you first need to identify specific characteristics and demographics of your potential customers. These characteristics could include:

- Age: The age range of your target market.
- Gender: The gender of your target market.
- Income: The income level of your target market.
- Location: The geographic location of your target market.
- Lifestyle: The lifestyle, interests and habits of your target market

- Education: The level of education of your target market
- Occupation: The occupation of your target market.
- Family status: Single, married, with children, without children.

This information can be gathered through various research methods such as customer surveys, focus groups, and market analysis. By having a general understanding of your target market, you can better tailor your product or service to meet their needs, and craft your message, marketing and advertising campaigns to appeal to them.

Once you have a general understanding of your target market, you can then segment it to identify sub-groups within your audience. This might include different segments with different needs or characteristics. For example, you may have one segment that is price-sensitive and another that is willing to pay a premium for a higher-quality product.

It is important to note that, as your business evolves and new trends or opportunities come up, you should continuously review and adjust your target market definition. This will ensure that you're reaching the right people, and that your message is still relevant.

Understanding customer needs

Understanding customer needs is a crucial step in developing a successful business strategy. It involves researching and analyzing the specific needs and desires of your target market in relation to your product or service. By understanding customer needs, you can create products and services that meet those needs, develop more effective marketing strategies, and create a more engaged customer base.

There are a variety of methods that can be used to understand customer needs. One approach is to conduct customer research, such as surveys, focus groups, and interviews. This can provide valuable insights into customer demographics, pain points, and the benefits and features that customers are looking for in a product or service.

Another approach is to gather customer feedback, this can be done through customer surveys, phone calls, social media and other means, this can provide insights into the customer experience and the performance of your products or services.

You can also use the customer journey map, it's a visual representation of the different stages a customer goes through when interacting with your business and it can help you understand the customer's needs, problems and pain points at each stage.

Additionally, you can observe the behavior of your customers, this can help you understand their needs in a more intuitive way, and in context, you may be able to identify patterns and trends that may not be obvious through other research methods.

Positioning and messaging

Positioning and messaging are crucial elements of a successful marketing strategy. Positioning refers to how a product or service is perceived by the target market, while messaging refers to the specific language and imagery used to communicate the value of the product or service. Together, positioning and messaging work to create a strong and consistent brand image that resonates with the target market.

To develop an effective positioning and messaging strategy, businesses must first understand their target market, as well as the competition in the market. This information will help to identify unique selling points, or what sets the product or service apart from the competition. By differentiating the product or service, businesses can create a unique position in the market.

Once a unique position has been established, businesses can then develop messaging that effectively communicates the value of the product or service to the target market. This messaging should align with the brand's overall positioning and convey the benefits and features of the product or service that are most important to the target market.

In order to develop a consistent messaging, it's important to create a messaging guide that outlines the key messaging points, the tone of voice, and the language that should be used when communicating with the target market. This guide will ensure that all communication is aligned and consistent.

Furthermore, it's important to evaluate the performance of the positioning and messaging strategy regularly, gathering customer feedback, monitor customer engagement and see if the messaging resonates well with the target market.

In summary, positioning and messaging are crucial elements of a successful marketing strategy. Businesses must first understand their target market and the competition in the market, in order to establish a unique position and develop messaging that effectively communicates the value of the product or service. A messaging guide will ensure that all communication is aligned and consistent, and performance evaluation will allow businesses to adjust the strategy as needed.

Adapting and growing

Adapting and growing is an essential part of any business strategy. It involves continuously monitoring and analyzing the performance of your business, identifying new opportunities and making changes as needed to ensure long-term success.

One important aspect of adapting and growing is staying informed about industry trends and changes in the market. This can be done by reading industry publications, attending trade shows and networking events, and keeping an eye on your competitors. By staying informed, you can identify new opportunities and make adjustments to your business strategy to take advantage of them.

Another key aspect of adapting and growing is monitoring the performance of your business, this can be done by analyzing key performance indicators (KPIs) such as sales, customer satisfaction, and website traffic. These indicators can provide valuable insights into the performance of your business and help you identify areas for improvement.

Another way to adapt and grow is to continuously gather customer feedback, which can help you identify areas of customer dissatisfaction and make necessary adjustments. It's also important to test and experiment with different strategies, promotions and marketing campaigns, this can help you understand what resonates with your target market and identify opportunities to improve your customer engagement.

Additionally, you can expand your target market by reaching new segments, this can be done by identifying new customer segments or by expanding your business offering to new geographic areas, this can help you tap into new markets and grow your revenue.

In summary, adapting and growing is essential for the long-term success of any business. By staying informed about industry trends, monitoring performance, gathering customer feedback, testing and experimenting, and expanding your target market, businesses can identify new opportunities and make necessary changes to ensure long-term success.

Chapter 4

Crafting a Business Model: Designing a sustainable and profitable business model.

Understanding business models

A business model is a plan for how a company generates revenue and creates value for its customers. It describes the way a company produces and delivers goods or services, as well as how it makes money from those activities. A well-designed business model is crucial for a company's long-term success as it defines the company's strategy for creating and capturing value.

There are many different types of business models, each with its own unique characteristics. Some common types of business models include:

- Product-based business model: This type of business model focuses on creating and selling physical products. Companies using this model typically manufacture or purchase products and then sell them to customers.
- Service-based business model: This type of business model focuses on providing services to customers. Examples include consulting, legal services, and repair services.
- Subscription-based business model: This type of business model involves charging customers a recurring fee for access to a service or product. Examples include streaming services and magazine subscriptions.
- Freemium business model: This type of business model involves offering a basic service or product for free, while charging for advanced features or additional services. Examples include free online games with paid upgrades and free email services with paid storage.
- Sharing economy business model: This type of business model allows individuals to share resources and assets through a platform or marketplace. Examples include Airbnb, Uber and TaskRabbit.
- Platform-based business model: This type of business model involves creating a platform that connects buyers and sellers, such as a

marketplace or social media network. Examples include Amazon, eBay, and LinkedIn.
- E-commerce business model: This type of business model focuses on selling goods or services through the internet, such as an online store or an app. Examples include Amazon, Alibaba and Etsy.

Once a business model has been chosen, it's important to continually evaluate and adapt it as needed. Market conditions and customer needs are constantly changing, so it's important for a business to be flexible and responsive to these changes in order to stay competitive.

One way to adapt and optimize the business model is to use experimentation and testing, this allows you to test new ideas and initiatives, and gather feedback from customers. This can help you identify new opportunities, improve customer engagement and increase revenue.

Another way to adapt is by monitoring key performance indicators (KPIs) and data analytics, this can help you understand how the business is performing, identify areas of improvement and make data-driven decisions.

Additionally, companies can also leverage digital technologies such as social media, e-commerce platforms, and mobile apps to reach and engage customers in new ways, and to create new revenue streams.

Another important aspect of adapting and growing your business model is being open to collaboration and partnerships. Collaborating with other companies, organizations, or individuals can bring new perspectives, resources and expertise that can help your business grow.

Partnerships can take many forms, such as joint ventures, licensing agreements, and strategic alliances. For example, a company in the technology industry might partner with a company in the healthcare industry to create new products or services that meet the needs of both industries.

Another example of partnership could be a company that specializes in the production of goods could partner with a company that specializes in logistics and distribution to streamline their supply chain.

Additionally, partnerships can be formed with suppliers, vendors and other businesses within the industry to leverage collective knowledge and resources, reduce costs and create new business opportunities.

Finally, another important aspect of adapting and growing your business model is being open to innovation and new ideas. Innovation can come in many forms, from product and service development, to process improvement, to business model design. By being open to new ideas, companies can stay ahead of the competition and meet the changing needs of customers.

One way to foster innovation is to create an environment that encourages experimentation, risk-taking and learning from failure. This can be achieved by setting up dedicated teams, programs or initiatives focused on innovation, and by providing resources and support for experimentation and testing.

Another way to foster innovation is to engage with customers, external partners, and other stakeholders through open innovation. This can include crowdsourcing, open research and development, and open sourcing. Engaging with external partners and stakeholders can help companies to identify new opportunities, gain new perspectives and access new resources and expertise.

Identifying revenue streams

Identifying revenue streams is an important step in developing a sustainable and profitable business model. A revenue stream is a source of income for a business, and there are many different types of revenue streams that a business can pursue.

One way to identify potential revenue streams is to conduct a thorough analysis of your business, identifying what products or services you currently offer, and how they are being sold. This can help you identify areas of your business that are already generating revenue and where there is room for growth.

Another way to identify revenue streams is to conduct customer research, this can help you understand your customers' needs, pain points, and what they are willing to pay for. This can help you identify potential revenue streams that align with your customer's needs and pain points.

Additionally, you can also look for opportunities to create new revenue streams by developing new products or services, expanding into new markets, or creating new distribution channels.

Once potential revenue streams have been identified, it's important to evaluate the potential profitability of each one, this can help you prioritize and focus on the revenue streams that have the highest potential for profitability.

After identifying and evaluating potential revenue streams, it's important to develop a plan for monetizing them. Monetizing a revenue stream involves creating a pricing strategy and sales plan for how a business will generate revenue from that stream.

When developing a pricing strategy, it's important to consider factors such as the cost of goods or services, the value that the customer receives, and the prices of competitors. It's also important to be flexible and adapt the pricing strategy as needed, for example, if the market conditions change, or if the costs of goods or services increase.

In addition to pricing, it's also important to develop a sales plan that outlines how the business will sell its products or services. This includes identifying target customers, creating a sales process, and developing a sales team. It's also important to have an effective marketing strategy that helps to attract customers and drive sales.

It's also important to consider the scalability and sustainability of your revenue stream, by studying the market trends, the demand for your products or services and its growth potential.

Another important aspect of identifying revenue streams is diversifying them. Diversifying revenue streams can provide a business with multiple sources of income, which can help to mitigate risk and improve financial stability.

For example, a business that solely relies on one product or service may experience a decline in sales if that product or service becomes less popular. However, a business that has diversified its revenue streams may still be able to generate income from other products or services, even if one of them experiences a decline in sales.

Additionally, diversifying revenue streams can also help a business to expand into new markets and reach new customers. This can help the business to identify new opportunities and grow its revenue.

Diversifying revenue streams can be achieved by adding new products or services, expanding into new markets, or creating new distribution channels.

Managing costs

Managing costs is an essential aspect of running a successful business. It involves identifying and controlling expenses in order to increase profitability and achieve long-term financial stability.

One way to manage costs is through cost cutting, which involves reducing expenses by finding more efficient ways to operate the business, or by eliminating unnecessary expenses. This can be achieved by streamlining operations, outsourcing non-core functions, and negotiating better terms with suppliers.

Another way to manage costs is through cost optimization, which involves finding ways to reduce costs without sacrificing the quality of the product or service. This can be achieved by adopting new technologies, automating processes, and improving supply chain efficiency.

It is also important to keep track of your expenses, by regularly monitoring and analyzing costs, businesses can identify areas where they are overspending and make adjustments as needed. This can be done by creating a budget and regularly comparing actual expenses to budgeted expenses.

Businesses can also use cost-benefit analysis, which involves evaluating the costs and benefits of a particular decision or project in order to determine its overall value. This can help to ensure that a business is spending its resources on the most important and profitable initiatives.

Another important aspect of managing costs is to be aware of fixed and variable costs. Fixed costs are expenses that remain the same regardless of the level of production or sales. These may include rent, salaries, and insurance. Variable costs, on the other hand, vary depending on the level of production or sales. Examples include raw materials, packaging and shipping costs.

It's important to be aware of the difference between fixed and variable costs because it can help the business to make better decisions and plan for future growth. For example, if a business is able to increase sales, the variable costs will also increase, but the fixed costs will remain the same. Therefore, it's important to consider the fixed costs when pricing products and services, as well as when projecting future revenues and expenses.

Another aspect of managing costs is to leverage economies of scale, which refers to the cost advantage that a business experiences when it increases production or sales. As a company produces more, the average cost per unit of output decreases, this is because fixed costs are spread out over a larger number of units. Therefore, it's important for the business to focus on growth in order to achieve economies of scale and to lower costs.

In conclusion, managing costs is a critical aspect of running a successful business, it's important for businesses to identify and control expenses in order to increase profitability and achieve long-term financial stability. By being aware of fixed and variable costs, leveraging economies of scale, and regularly monitoring expenses, businesses can make better decisions and plan for growth and success.

Building a scalable business model

Building a scalable business model is a key aspect of creating a sustainable and profitable company. A scalable business model is one that can handle an increase in customer demand or growth without a corresponding increase in costs. This allows a business to grow and expand without having to continually re-invest in infrastructure, systems, and processes.

One way to build a scalable business model is by leveraging technology. Automation and digital technologies can help to streamline operations, reduce costs, and increase efficiency. For example, an e-commerce platform can allow a business to expand into new markets and reach more customers without having to invest in physical storefronts or distribution centers.

Another way to build a scalable business model is by creating a network effect. Network effects occur when the value of a product or service increases as more people use it. For example, the more people who use a social media platform, the more valuable it becomes, both for the users and for the business.

Additionally, building a scalable business model can also be achieved by using a franchise or licensing model, This allows other businesses to operate under the company's name and systems, thereby expanding the company's reach without having to invest additional capital or resources in the new locations.

Another key aspect of building a scalable business model is to focus on recurring revenue streams. Recurring revenue streams are those that generate income on a consistent basis, such as subscription-based models, memberships or retaining customers through a service. This can provide a predictable and consistent source of income for the business, which can help to support growth and expansion.

Furthermore, building a scalable business model also involves creating a flexible organization structure that can adapt to changing market conditions and customer needs. This means having a management team that can quickly make decisions and implement changes as needed, as well as having processes in place to gather customer feedback and respond to it.

It is also important to establish strong relationships with suppliers and partners, this can help you to negotiate better prices and take advantage of economies of scale. Strong relationships with suppliers and partners can also provide access to new resources and expertise that can help a business to grow and adapt.

Finally, Having a scalable business model also means having the ability to measure, track and analyze key performance indicators (KPIs) that can provide insights into the performance of the business and opportunities for improvement. This includes measuring customer acquisition costs, lifetime customer value, and customer retention rates among others.

Monitoring and adapting

Monitoring and adapting are crucial aspects of running a successful business. They involve regularly evaluating the performance of a business and making adjustments as needed to improve performance, achieve goals, and stay competitive.

One important aspect of monitoring and adapting is regularly reviewing key performance indicators (KPIs) such as financial performance, customer satisfaction, and employee engagement. This can help a business to identify areas where it is performing well and where it needs to improve.

Another important aspect of monitoring and adapting is staying informed about industry trends and changes in the market. This can help a business to identify new opportunities, anticipate challenges, and make strategic decisions.

It's also important to gather feedback from customers and employees, and using it to make improvements. This can help a business to understand how its products or services are perceived by customers, identify areas where they may need improvement, and stay responsive to the needs of its customers.

Additionally, it's important to regularly review and assess the business's overall strategy, and make changes as needed to stay aligned with the company's goals and to adapt to the changing business environment.

Monitoring and adapting also involve being open to new ideas and experimenting with new approaches. This means having a culture that encourages experimentation, learning and taking calculated risks. This can help a business to identify new opportunities and stay ahead of its competitors.

It's also important to have a system in place for continuous improvement, by regularly reviewing processes, procedures and policies, a business can identify inefficiencies, and make changes that can lead to improved performance and cost savings. This can be achieved by using tools such as Lean Six Sigma, which is a process improvement methodology.

Flexibility is another key aspect of monitoring and adapting, being able to adjust plans, pivot the business model, or change direction when needed. This is critical to being able to respond to changes in the market, new competitors, or shifts in consumer behavior, this can be difficult, but it's necessary for the survival and growth of the business.

Finally, monitoring and adapting also involve having a team that is willing to be proactive and take initiative. This means having a team that is not afraid to take risks, think creatively and come up with new solutions when faced with challenges. A team that is proactive, flexible and adaptable will be better equipped to handle changes and find new opportunities.

Chapter 5

Building a Team: Assembling the right people to bring your vision to life.

Defining roles and responsibilities

Defining roles and responsibilities is a crucial step in building a team that can help bring a business's vision to life. It involves identifying the key roles and responsibilities that are necessary to achieve the business's goals and determining the skills, knowledge, and experience that are required for each role.

When defining roles and responsibilities, it's important to consider the overall goals of the business and how each role fits into the bigger picture. This includes identifying the key functions that need to be performed and the tasks that are required to achieve them.

It's also important to consider the interdependencies between different roles and responsibilities, and how they interact and support one another. This can help to ensure that each team member has a clear understanding of what is expected of them and how their role fits into the broader goals of the business.

Once the roles and responsibilities have been defined, it's important to develop detailed job descriptions that outline the specific responsibilities, required qualifications, and experience for each role. This can help to ensure that the team members are aware of what is expected of them and can help in the recruitment process as well.

It's also important to continuously review and evaluate the roles and responsibilities as the business evolves and adapts to changing market conditions. This includes considering new opportunities, challenges and re-evaluating which roles and responsibilities are most important for the current and future state of the business.

It's also important to ensure that the roles and responsibilities are clearly communicated to the team members. This includes providing them with detailed job descriptions, as well as regular updates and feedback on their performance. Clear communication can help to ensure that each team member is aware of what is expected of them, and can also help to foster a sense of shared purpose and direction within the team.

To support the team, creating a clear and transparent structure for the team is important, this can be achieved through creating an org chart that clearly communicates the reporting structure, chain of command and key decision making process, This can help to ensure that everyone knows who they should report to and who to go to with different types of questions, requests and issues.

In addition to clear communication and structure, it's also important to establish performance metrics and regularly evaluate the performance of the team. This can help to identify areas of improvement, and also to celebrate successes and achievements. Having these metrics in place can also be used to communicate performance with the team members and identify areas where they may require more training or support.

Another aspect of building a team is providing clear onboarding process, this helps new hires to quickly understand the company's culture, values, expectations, and goals. This can also be supported by providing them with necessary materials, equipment and information, as well as making sure that there is a designated person responsible for their orientation and integration into the team.

Recruiting the right people

Recruiting the right people is a critical step in building a team that can help bring a business's vision to life. It involves identifying the most qualified and suitable candidates for the available roles.

The first step in recruiting the right people is to develop a clear job description that outlines the specific responsibilities, required qualifications, and experience for the role. This can help to attract the most suitable candidates, and also to provide a benchmark for evaluating candidates during the recruitment process.

Once the job description is developed, it can be posted on job boards, or shared with recruitment agencies, professional networks, and through employee referrals. This can help to reach a large pool of candidates, and also to identify candidates who might not have actively applied for the role.

When evaluating candidates, it's important to consider their qualifications, experience, and skills, as well as their cultural fit with the organization. This can include looking at their values, work style and overall personality, how they would fit in with the team and contribute to the company culture.

It's also important to conduct thorough interviews, reference checks, and background screenings to ensure that each candidate is a good fit for the role and the company. This can help to minimize the risk of hiring a candidate who might not be able to perform the job, or who may not be a good fit for the organization.

Finally, it's important to have a clear process for selecting and onboarding new hires, this can include providing a clear offer letter that outlines the terms of the employment, and providing them with the necessary materials, equipment and information to get started.

Building a strong culture

Building a strong culture is an important aspect of building a team that can help bring a business's vision to life. A strong culture can help to create a sense of shared purpose and direction, foster a sense of belonging and commitment, and ultimately improve the performance and productivity of the team.

One key aspect of building a strong culture is establishing a shared vision and set of values for the team. This includes identifying the core purpose and goals of the organization, as well as the values and principles that guide the behavior of the team members. Having a shared vision and set of values can help to create a sense of direction and purpose for the team, and can also serve as a basis for decision-making and problem-solving.

It's important that the vision and values are communicated clearly to the team members, this can be achieved through various methods such as company meetings, email communications, internal newsletter and even through the company website. This helps team members to understand and align with the company's mission and values and also ensure that these are integrated into their daily work and decision making process.

Leadership is also important in building a strong culture, this starts from the top with the company's leaders setting the tone and leading by example. They should role model the values and behaviors they expect from the team members, this includes, ethical behavior, open communication and a positive attitude.

Creating a culture of inclusivity and diversity is also important, it helps to foster an environment where everyone feels valued and respected. This includes creating a welcoming environment for all team members, regardless of their background, identity, and experiences. This can also help to improve the performance and productivity of the team by leveraging the unique perspectives and ideas of different team members.

Providing training and development

Providing training and development opportunities is an essential aspect of building a team that can help bring a business's vision to life. It is important to continuously invest in the team members' growth and development, as this can help to keep them motivated, engaged and improve their performance in their roles.

Training and development can include a wide range of activities such as formal courses, workshops, webinars, on-the-job training, and mentoring programs. It should be tailored to the individual needs of each team member, taking into consideration their current role, career aspirations, and areas for improvement.

One effective way to provide training and development is through a combination of both formal and informal learning. Formal learning can include attending workshops, conferences, or taking online courses to acquire new skills and knowledge. While informal learning can include things like job shadowing, attending internal meetings, or participating in cross-functional teams. This can help team members to learn from their peers and gain insights from other teams and departments, which can help to broaden their perspective and improve their understanding of the organization as a whole.

Providing access to learning resources such as books, articles, videos, and webinars is also important, this provides team members with a self-paced and flexible way to learn new skills and stay updated on industry trends.

In addition to training and development, performance management is also important, this includes setting performance expectations, providing regular feedback and coaching, and conducting performance evaluations. This can help to identify areas for improvement, as well as to celebrate successes and achievements.

It is also important to provide opportunities for professional development and career growth. This can include things like offering opportunities for advancement, creating clear career paths, and providing mentoring and coaching. By providing opportunities for professional development and career growth, team members can feel more motivated, engaged, and committed to the organization.

Furthermore, It is also important to evaluate and measure the effectiveness of training and development programs, this can help to identify what worked well and what needs improvement. Gathering feedback from the team members and tracking progress can help to measure the effectiveness of the training and development programs and adjust as needed.

Another important aspect of providing training and development is making sure that it's accessible to all team members, regardless of their role, background or level within the organization. By providing opportunities for everyone to learn and grow, you can help to create a more inclusive and equitable environment where everyone can thrive.

Finally, it is important to provide recognition and rewards for learning and development, this can help to motivate team members to continue learning and growing. This can include offering bonuses, promotions, or other incentives for completing training or achieving certain milestones

Communication and collaboration

Effective communication and collaboration are critical aspects of building a team that can help bring a business's vision to life. They are essential for building trust, fostering teamwork, and ensuring that everyone is on the same page.

Effective communication is important for ensuring that all team members are aware of what is expected of them, and that they are able to provide and receive feedback in a constructive manner. This can be achieved through regular team meetings, one-on-one conversations, or through online communication tools.

Clear communication of expectations and goals is also essential, this can help to ensure that everyone is aware of what needs to be done, and also helps to minimize confusion or misunderstandings. It's important that all team members understand their roles and responsibilities and can access the information they need to perform their jobs well.

Creating a culture of open communication can also help to create a more positive work environment where team members feel comfortable bringing forward their ideas, concerns and feedback.

Effective collaboration involves working together towards a common goal, this can be achieved through creating a collaborative work environment and fostering a culture of teamwork. Collaboration can also be enhanced through the use of project management tools and technologies, this can help to promote teamwork, improve communication and make it easier for team members to share information, collaborate and track progress.

In addition to collaboration within the team, it's important to foster a culture of cross-functional collaboration. This includes working with other teams and departments in the organization to share knowledge, skills and resources. This can help to improve efficiency, foster innovation, and create a more cohesive and effective organization.

Effective communication and collaboration also help to build a culture of trust, where team members feel comfortable sharing their thoughts, concerns and ideas, and feel that their contributions are valued. Trust can help to foster a positive work environment, improve morale and increase productivity.

Furthermore, effective communication and collaboration can also help to improve problem-solving and decision-making. By working together and sharing different perspectives, team members can come up with more innovative solutions and make better decisions.

It's also important to recognize the different communication styles and needs of team members, this can help to create a more inclusive and respectful work environment. This can be done by providing training on effective communication and collaboration, and also by promoting open and respectful communication and feedback.

Moreover, it's important to have a system in place for managing conflicts, this can be done through regular team meetings, open communication, and establishing clear policies and procedures for resolving conflicts.

Managing and motivating the team

Managing and motivating a team is an essential aspect of building a team that can help bring a business's vision to life. It involves setting clear expectations, providing regular feedback, and recognizing and rewarding good performance.

One important aspect of managing and motivating a team is setting clear expectations and goals. This includes communicating what is expected of team members, and providing them with the necessary resources and support to meet those expectations. Having clearly defined goals can also help team members understand how their work fits into the bigger picture and contribute to the success of the organization.

Providing regular feedback is also important, this includes both positive and constructive feedback, it can help to improve performance, and also to keep team members on track. Feedback can be provided through regular team meetings, one-on-one conversations, or through performance evaluations.

Recognizing and rewarding good performance is another important aspect of managing and motivating a team. This can be done by recognizing individual achievements and contributions, and also by providing rewards such as bonuses, promotions, or other incentives. Recognition and rewards can help to increase motivation and engagement, and can also help to improve retention.

Leadership is also important in managing and motivating a team, this starts from the top with the company's leaders setting the tone and leading by example. They should role model the values and behaviours they expect from the team members, this includes, ethical behavior, open communication and a positive attitude.

Fostering a positive work environment and culture can also help to improve motivation and engagement, this includes creating a welcoming environment for all team members, regardless of their background, identity, and experiences. Additionally, promoting open communication and providing opportunities for learning and development can also help to improve motivation and engagement.

Measuring and evaluating team performance

Measuring and evaluating team performance is an important aspect of building a team that can help bring a business's vision to life. It involves assessing how well the team is performing against established goals and objectives, and taking steps to address any issues or challenges that arise.

One key aspect of measuring and evaluating team performance is setting clear goals and objectives. This includes identifying what the team needs to achieve, and determining how success will be measured. These goals and objectives should be aligned with the overall goals and objectives of the organization.

Another important aspect of measuring and evaluating team performance is tracking progress and collecting data. This includes monitoring key performance indicators (KPIs) such as productivity, customer satisfaction, and employee engagement, and using this data to identify trends and areas for improvement.

Regular performance evaluations are also important, this can be done through performance appraisals, or through more frequent check-ins, it provides an opportunity to provide feedback, identify areas for improvement, and recognize achievements and progress.

It's important to gather feedback from team members, this can be done through surveys, focus groups, or one-on-one conversations. Feedback can help to identify areas of strengths, as well as areas that need improvement.

Finally, it's important to take action to address any issues or challenges that arise, this can include providing additional training or support, re-aligning goals and objectives, and making changes to processes or systems. It's important to track progress and adjust as needed, this will help to ensure continuous improvement and success.

Chapter 6

Raising Capital: Securing funding and financial support for your business.

Understanding your funding options

Raising capital is an essential aspect of building a business, and it requires a thorough understanding of the various funding options available. Some of the most common funding options include equity funding, debt funding, and crowdfunding.

Equity funding involves selling shares in the company to investors in exchange for capital. This is typically done through a process called fundraising, and can include things like angel investing, venture capital, or an initial public offering (IPO). One of the main benefits of equity funding is that it doesn't require the repayment of the funds raised and also that it allows the business to benefit from the expertise and resources of the investors.

Debt funding, on the other hand, involves borrowing money from lenders and is usually in the form of a loan. This type of funding is usually used for short-term needs, such as working capital or to finance a specific project. The main advantage of debt funding is that it allows businesses to access funds without giving up ownership or control of the company.

Crowdfunding is another popular option for raising capital, it allows businesses to raise money from a large number of individuals, usually through online platforms. Crowdfunding can take various forms such as rewards-based crowdfunding, equity crowdfunding, or debt crowdfunding. The main advantage of crowdfunding is that it allows businesses to tap into a large number of investors, and can also help to create a buzz and build a community of supporters around the business.

Preparing for a funding round

Once you have a clear understanding of the funding options available, the next step is to prepare for a funding round. This includes putting together a compelling business plan, assembling a strong team, and building a solid financial track record.

A well-written business plan should clearly outline the value proposition of the business, describe the market opportunity, and provide a detailed financial plan and projections. It's also important to have a clear understanding of the competitive landscape and be able to articulate how the business will differentiate itself from the competition.

Assembling a strong team is also important, this includes having a dedicated and experienced management team, as well as a board of advisors or directors with relevant experience and expertise. Investors will also want to see a solid financial track record, so it's important to have accurate and up-to-date financial statements, as well as a clear understanding of key financial metrics such as revenue, profitability, and cash flow.

Securing funding

Once you have a solid business plan, a strong team, and a solid financial track record, it's time to start the process of securing funding. This can include reaching out to potential investors, attending networking events, and leveraging online platforms to connect with potential investors.

Before reaching out to investors, it's important to have a clear idea of what type of funding you're seeking, and what kind of investor would be the best fit for your business. This includes understanding the investor's investment criteria, investment philosophy, and areas of expertise.

Networking events such as startup competitions, pitch events, and investor conferences can be a great way to connect with potential investors. It's important to be prepared with a clear and compelling pitch, and to follow up with investors after the event.

Online platforms such as AngelList, Seedrs and Crowdfunder can also be used to connect with potential investors. These platforms allow businesses to create an online profile, share their business plan and financials, and connect with potential investors.

Finally, it's important to be prepared to negotiate terms and deal structure with investors, this can include things like equity, valuation, and control. It's important to have a clear understanding of what you are willing to accept and what you are not willing to compromise on.

In conclusion, Raising capital is an essential aspect of building a business and requires a thorough understanding of the funding options available, preparing a compelling business plan, assembling a strong team and building a solid financial track record. Networking, leveraging online platforms and negotiating with the investor are also important. By understanding these steps and being prepared, you increase the chances of successfully securing the funding needed to bring your business vision to life.

Chapter 7

Marketing and Branding: Creating a strong brand and effective marketing strategy.

The Importance of Marketing and Branding

Marketing and branding are essential aspects of building a successful business. Marketing is the process of promoting and selling products or services, while branding is the process of creating a unique identity and reputation for a business. Together, marketing and branding can help to create a strong and recognizable brand, increase awareness and interest in the business, and ultimately drive sales.

Creating a strong brand starts with developing a clear and compelling brand message and identity.

This includes creating a unique name, logo, and visual identity for the business. It's also important to identify the target market, and to create a message that speaks directly to them.

Developing an effective marketing strategy is also important. This includes researching the target market, identifying the unique value proposition of the business, and creating a plan for promoting the business. The most common marketing channels include digital marketing, such as social media and email marketing, content marketing, paid advertising, and events.

It's important to set measurable goals, and track the performance of marketing activities, this will help to understand which marketing activities are effective and which need to be improved.

Branding and marketing also play a key role in building and maintaining customer loyalty. A strong brand can help to create trust and a positive reputation for the business, which in turn can lead to repeat customers and positive word-of-mouth.

Implementing and Managing Marketing and Branding Efforts

Implementing a marketing and branding strategy can be challenging, but with the right approach, it can be done effectively. One important step is to establish a budget and allocate resources accordingly. This includes not just monetary resources but also human resources as well as time and effort.

Another important step is to create a content calendar, that aligns with the business's overall goals and objectives, this will help to ensure that all marketing activities are focused, consistent, and in line with the overall strategy. This can also be helpful in tracking progress, adjusting and improving the marketing strategy, when needed.

Creating a dedicated marketing team, with a clear organizational structure and roles, can also help to improve the efficiency and effectiveness of marketing and branding efforts. This can include dedicated marketing professionals and also training internal team members to take on marketing responsibilities.

Effective marketing and branding also requires active monitoring, measurement, and analysis of the results of campaigns. This can include tracking metrics such as website traffic, social media engagement, and conversions. It's also important to collect customer feedback and to incorporate that feedback into the marketing and branding strategy.

Another important aspect of implementing and managing marketing and branding efforts is to use the right tools and technologies to streamline the process and maximize results. This includes using marketing automation software, analytics and data visualization tools, social media management tools, and CRM systems.

Marketing automation software can help businesses to automate repetitive tasks such as email marketing and lead nurturing, freeing up time and resources for other marketing activities. Analytics and data visualization tools can help businesses to track and analyze the performance of marketing campaigns and make data-driven decisions.

Social media management tools can help businesses to track and analyze the performance of social media campaigns and make data-driven decisions. CRM systems can help businesses to manage customer relationships, track customer interactions, and analyze customer data to better understand customer needs and preferences.

Another key aspect of managing marketing and branding efforts is to ensure that they are aligned with the company's overall mission, vision, and values. This includes ensuring that all marketing and branding efforts reflect the company's unique value proposition, promote its strengths, and communicate its unique brand identity.

Finally, it's important to have a clear process in place for managing and updating branding elements, such as the company's logo, website, and other visual elements. This process should include guidelines for how and when to update branding elements, as well as a process for getting approval from key stakeholders.

Leveraging Public Relations to Build Brand Reputation

Public relations, also known as PR, is an important aspect of building and maintaining a positive brand reputation. Public relations involves managing and communicating with the media, customers, and other stakeholders to shape public perception of a business.

A strong public relations strategy can help to build and maintain a positive reputation for the business, by highlighting the business's strengths, achievements, and value proposition, while addressing any potential issues or challenges.

One key aspect of public relations is to actively engage with the media and create a positive relationship with them. This can include pitching story ideas, providing quotes and expert commentary, and proactively addressing any negative coverage.

Another important aspect of public relations is to actively manage the company's online presence, which includes monitoring and managing customer reviews and feedback, responding to comments and complaints, and proactively addressing any issues that may arise.

Another key aspect of public relations is to leverage events, such as product launches, press conferences and other events, to build a positive relationship with the media and to generate positive coverage for the business.

Additionally, Public Relations can also support to build a strong relationship with the community and help to create a positive impact in the society, through partnerships and corporate social responsibility initiatives, it will not only help the business to connect with customers, stakeholders and other business, but it will also help to improve reputation, establish trust and show that the business is making a positive impact in the society.

Another important aspect of public relations is the use of storytelling to communicate the business's message, mission, and values. By using storytelling, businesses can effectively communicate their unique value proposition, showcase their achievements and create a human connection with their target audience. This can be done through different formats such as written articles, videos, podcasts, and more.

Measuring and evaluating the results of public relations efforts is also crucial. This can include tracking media coverage, social media engagement, website traffic, and any other metrics that may be relevant to the business. By regularly tracking and analyzing these metrics, businesses can identify which public relations efforts are working and which need to be improved.

As part of the public relations strategy, crisis management is also an important aspect. Crisis management plans provide a framework for identifying and mitigating potential risks, and respond to negative or unexpected events that could harm the business's reputation, so it's important to have a plan in place, and know how to execute it, to minimize damage and maintain trust.

It's also important to keep in mind that Public Relations should be an ongoing effort, not a one-time campaign. Businesses should constantly be looking for new opportunities to engage with the media, customers, and other stakeholders, and be prepared to adapt and adjust their public relations strategy as needed.

Building Influencer Marketing Strategies

Influencer marketing is a type of marketing that leverages the power of social media influencers to reach and connect with the target audience. Influencer marketing is an effective way to increase brand awareness, build credibility and trust, and drive sales.

The first step in building an influencer marketing strategy is to identify the appropriate influencers to work with. This includes researching the influencer's audience, niche, and brand alignment. It's important to find influencers who have a significant following in your target market, and whose personal brand aligns with the business's brand values and message.

Once the influencers have been identified, the next step is to create a campaign that aligns with the business's overall marketing goals and objectives. This includes creating a clear and compelling message, determining the appropriate content format, and setting measurable campaign goals.

It's also important to establish clear guidelines and guidelines for the influencer to follow, to ensure that the campaign aligns with the business's overall message and stays within the desired parameters, this will also help to avoid any potential conflict of interest or negative impact.

Measuring and evaluating the results of influencer marketing campaigns is also important, this can include tracking metrics such as website traffic, social media engagement, and conversions. This will help the business to understand which campaigns are working and which need to be improved, which can be used as a basis for future campaigns.

Managing and Leveraging Brand Ambassadors

Brand ambassadors are individuals who have a genuine interest and connection with a brand, and who are willing to promote it to their own network of friends, family, and followers. Leveraging brand ambassadors can be an effective way to increase brand awareness and drive sales, by tapping into their personal networks and reaching new audiences.

The first step in building a brand ambassadors program is to identify potential brand ambassadors. This can include current customers, fans of the brand, or even employees who have a personal connection with the brand.

Once the brand ambassadors have been identified, the next step is to establish a clear set of guidelines and expectations for their involvement in the program. This should include information on what they are expected to do, how often they are expected to participate, and how they will be compensated.

It's also important to provide brand ambassadors with the resources and support they need to effectively promote the brand. This can include marketing materials, product samples, and access to exclusive events and promotions.

Measuring and evaluating the performance of brand ambassadors is also important. This can include tracking metrics such as website traffic, social media engagement, and conversions. By regularly tracking and analyzing these metrics, businesses can understand which brand ambassadors are most effective and allocate resources accordingly.

Finally, it's important to recognize and reward brand ambassadors for their participation. This can include offering discounts, exclusive promotions, or even publicly recognizing them for their efforts. This can help to build a strong relationship with the brand ambassadors and incentivize them to continue promoting the brand.

Conclusion

Staying true to your vision, being agile and adaptable in the face of change, and continuing to innovate and grow.

One of the keys to business success is staying true to your vision, while remaining agile and adaptable in the face of change. This requires a combination of a clear vision, a well thought-out strategy, and the ability to adapt and evolve as the market and competitive landscape change.

Having a clear vision for the business, and a strategy to achieve it, is essential. This vision should be well-articulated and communicated to the team, and should be used to guide decision-making and shape the overall direction of the business.

However, even with a clear vision and strategy, businesses must be prepared to adapt and evolve as the market and competitive landscape change. This requires being open to new ideas, being willing to experiment, and having the ability to pivot when necessary.

Being agile also means being willing to take calculated risks, and being prepared to fail fast and learn from those failures. It's important to try new things, to test new markets and to implement new technologies, but if things don't go as planned, it's better to learn from it and move on quickly.

Another important aspect of staying true to your vision, being agile and adaptable in the face of change, is to continue to innovate and grow. This requires constantly looking for new opportunities, staying ahead of the curve and continuously improving. Businesses that are able to continuously innovate and grow are more likely to survive and thrive in a constantly changing market.

Lastly, fostering a culture of learning, experimentation and adaptability can help to support the organization in staying true to its vision, being agile and adaptable in the face of change, and continuing to innovate and grow. By encouraging experimentation, new ideas and learning from failure, the organization will be more resilient and be able to pivot when needed, and continue to improve over time.

When it comes to staying true to your vision, being agile and adaptable, and continuing to innovate and grow, it's important to remember that there is no one-size-fits-all approach. Every business is different, and what works for one business may not work for another.

Here are a few tips to keep in mind as you navigate these challenges:

1. Keep your vision at the forefront of your mind: Your vision should be the guiding light that helps you make difficult decisions and stay focused on your goals. Make sure it's communicated clearly to everyone on your team and that everyone understands their role in helping you achieve it.
2. Embrace change and be open to new ideas: The world is constantly changing, and businesses that are able to adapt and evolve are the ones that thrive. Be open to new ideas and be willing to experiment with new strategies and technologies.

3. Be willing to take risks: Innovation often requires taking risks. It's important to balance the potential rewards with the potential risks and make informed decisions about when to take a leap of faith.
4. Learn from your failures: Failure is an inevitable part of business, and it's important to be able to learn from your mistakes. Be prepared to pivot when necessary, and use your failures as a learning opportunity to improve your strategy.
5. Continuously monitor and assess your progress: Keep track of your progress and make adjustments as needed. This will help you to identify what is working and what is not, and make the necessary adjustments to stay on course towards your vision.

www.ingramcontent.com/pod-product-compliance
Lightning Source LLC
Chambersburg PA
CBHW071126240526
45465CB00024B/1402